The trap.

The trap

Juan Manuel Ramírez Magallón

Published by No, 2023.

THE TRAP

First edition. November 15, 2023.

Copyright © 2023 Juan Manuel Ramírez Magallón.

ISBN: 979-8223342038

Written by Juan Manuel Ramírez Magallón.

Table of Contents

By Juan Manuel Ramírez Magallón

First edition 2023
Magallón, Juan M.
The trap / Juan Manuel Ramirez Magallón,
Mexico 2023

D.R. ©2023 Juan Manuel Ramírez Magallón
Independencia S/N new colony Aquila, Aquila, Michoacán, México, C.P. 60870. Cell 3121349204

Introduction

It is a free work, the story of charcoal, a child who thinks that the world is a trap, into which the human falls and makes him captive, when he develops his story he shows his concerns lived in the countryside and the city, the same ones that marked their existence.

Carboncito tries to understand the world from his own perspective, he falls into many unknowns and worries that make him say a variety of wrong things and some correct ones.

Carboncito learned the work of the countryside and aroused affection for the natural environment, then he moved to the city and discovered another world, many doubts and concerns about the behaviors that he observed in the city.

The origin of carbonite.

I tell you that in a distant December a child was born and they call him "carbonito", he is the child who said that everything is a trap, he shared his adventures with his dripping cousins, from that ranchería and saw the world in childhood from the point of view subjective, referring to the objects and behaviors that hook us from the moment we are born and even before we are born, because they say that there are innate forces that accompany each person and determine them to certain behaviors, but it could be a trap.

I had the hypothesis that from the moment you generate a being, you destine it to be exposed to many traps. First of all, a particle enters a trap where it is encapsulated and divided in such a way that it gives rise to a female or male embryo, after being born. they catch on designs and colors; incidental entities that make free people determined, according to their encounter with the outside is the behavior they develop.

The trap that hooks people is the conscious and unconscious imitation of their parents, siblings and social environment, stunting the ability to be free, violating self-determination and obstructing one's own criteria, making a being subject to profane and petty vices.

That personality trap consists of my parents giving me a name, of which I am ashamed and although I am not the name, it damages me and determines me to an affront that I cannot bear, for such a situation I prefer to be called carboncito.

Today I started an uncomfortable conversation with my mother in which she told me with a bossy voice:

—Rufino Austreberto del Niño Jesús, fix your notebooks for school! Hearing this phrase makes my stomach cramp and makes me want to run to the bathroom. But the figure of my mother can help me, she makes me answer with respect and even with rebellion, but with respect she answered him:

— I don't like going to school! – Charcoal exclaimed, frowning with some anger. "They don't teach me anything, I already know everything the teacher says and it only makes me bored," my mother could not remain silent upon hearing such a refutation and she replied:

—Why don't you like going to school? —My mother demands me very strongly, almost overpowering her voice.

—Because the uniform looks like a prisoner, a worker, or a third-rate police officer. I referred to the uniform in a derogatory way, although inside I heard the voice of my duty to attend school, and my complacent mother answered me saying:

— Do you want them to change the color or style? – My loving mother gave me options without predicting the insolence that came out of my mouth:

— I want there to be no uniform, the classes to be free and without reluctance due to age, these were extreme demands for an eight-year-old child, from that age it generated conflicts for my poor mother that came out of her voice:

—So you want to do whatever you want. And with insistence and measure I answered:

—It's not about that, mom! —My mother didn't take a second to answer me with a question:

- So? — Tempers were beginning to get out of control, so I decided to be a little more objective and clearly define what I thought would be the right thing to do and I contributed:

— It is about the system changing the form and substance of the way of educating childhood, so that youth and old age are different, the damage is done to children, then adults return it to children and it becomes in a never-ending vice - my mother seemed to accept and not my voice, she felt that she was blocked and concluded by giving her resolution:

—You have to do what I tell you without refuting—My mother insisted, but I contradicted again, telling my mother:

— You are a product of a system, that system that if you are different they eliminate you. It does not allow what is different or what is not profit or merchandise. That's what it consists of: either they sell you or they buy you, but they don't allow you to really be a person. I noticed concern on my mother's face and then I heard her say:

—Where do you get so many things from, son? —I thought quickly and discovered that my mother wanted to know the source of my rebellion and I told her:

— I'm not going to discover my ally, I want to know if you could tell the system that there is room for different people, those people who are not hooked on the physical but on the metaphysical, the symbolic, the truly valuable. Those things that the profane world does not reach. And while I was taking off my philosophical flight, my mother's voice landed on me like a cannon shot:

—Son, beings have to subject themselves to what there is!

I clung to wanting to make my mother understand, but I think that her poor academic level was surpassed by the arrogance of that kid who read her father's books, red books that the system considers terrorism and bad influence. To which I urged exclaiming:

—Exactly that is why I avoid the trap of saying that I am subject to the guidelines of what is established!

In my brain as a child, the rebellion of not accepting manipulation of any kind was hatched. That day it became a little tense because my mother doesn't like innovative ideas and she reprimands me in the following way:

The trap consists of getting hooked on rebellion, on that rebellion that sees everything with negative eyes, it doesn't let you see that adults are right and if I tell you it's for a reason.

My mother spoke as if he were one of those dictators from democratic republics and I questioned him again with my thoughts:

— I don't like that something, you could be more clear and concise in your words. – I replied, becoming the Little Charcoal boy, the darkest in the history of humanity. While my mother struggled to reconcile with patience and she answered me:

- My son, I'm not giving you orders to bother you! I do it because I love you and the times I have hit you it is because I love you.

That love of my mother was a very particular love and my dark sarcasm could not be missing:

— Yes, you love me very much, you have hit me with the whip, with the rope, with the ranger, with the güinar broom and even with sticks like snakes.

My gestures were not very kind and I planted my complaint:
- Yes, you love me, mother.

And I saw my mother break her temper a little and she wanted to mediate between the parties trying to apologize:

—Son, forgive me for all the frustration and anger that I have vented on you, it is due to lack of control and you know that those hyenas of your aunts have provoked a lot of fury and hysteria in me.

With a little regret, my mother said, somewhat penitently. Upon hearing this, I replied with great condolences:

— I forgive you mother because I understand that you don't know what you're doing.

I saw myself as Jesus Christ nailed to the cross, a victim, and my mother replied:

- I know what I'm doing son, I have done you a lot of harm, so much so that the blows I have given you I fear that you will give them to the world, that rebellion and negative attitude is nothing other than the results of my bad education towards you . You do not have the capacity to understand it and because of my ill will I have not been able to stop hurting you.

Without allowing him to continue speaking, I interrupted him:

- Mother! I am going to begin the transformation and combat my bad behavior, but I ask you only one thing: Do not apply violence to me again, in any way. Remember the times you have scolded me for not doing your homework—, I told my mother with great confidence. She answered me with some remorse:

— I promise you my little one that mine will never be the same attitude again, today that we miss your father we are going to do things well, away from your father's people. – My mother, with deep sadness, wiped away some tears with her black mourning suit, which she wears daily after several years of mourning.

While I took advantage of seeing my mother devastated, she answered him with a certain haughtiness:

— I agree mom! We are restructuring our family. Because the only way to move forward will be through our own means. I kept throwing away the altero tortillas that my mother made with corn from our production.

- Yes, son, your grandfather didn't want to help me - my mother replied - I asked him for help for you and he didn't want to help me, God bless him, he wants to force me to join his religion in exchange for helping me with your support. – My mother's broken tone of voice gave her enough credibility and aroused enough anger in me to go and complain to my grandfather.

—Mom, we don't take anything from my grandfather, may God put it on his list, we are going to fight for ourselves and show him that we can do it alone.

— Yes, my child, we are going to work the land together and take care of the planting, we will increase the lot of cows and pastures.

—And my father's lands? –Carboncito asked very demandingly.

—Your father's lands have been distributed among your people.

— How unfortunate, the curse is going to fall on your products and goods.

—Do not wish harm on anyone son, they are slaves of ignorance and evil.

—But mother, we worked those lands with my father, I have grown up in them, they have the essence of my father, his struggle and his desires.

—Son, your father is no longer here, but we will start again without him.

— Okay mom.

Between biting into the tortilla and weighing the beans, he carried mixed feelings to my subconscious. How was it possible? It was the question that repeated the most in my mind. The evil of adults against the most vulnerable, against a widow and five children, is very great. While my sisters and brothers continued to fight to study and work, I continued to deny the misfortune.

That day I went to school and encountered many negative feelings. The children made fun of me because they killed my father and the pain did not let me continue that day in the classroom, the teacher hit my brother with a ruler for fighting in defense of his honor and the children take advantage of our pain to make fun . My mother is working the land and we go to where she is:

—Mom, the children fought with us. -my mother hugs us-

— Don't worry children, we are going to leave this place.

—But mother, I can defend myself, if I can't with my fists, lend me the 45.

- Never! You will not stain your hands with blood, honor can be defended in a thousand ways and one is by walking away, because, in the end, history will speak of us. – Those were my mother's words while she cleaned her face with a red handkerchief.

"If we leave here, they won't pay us for the land and they will see us as cowards," I replied to my mother, full of anger.

- It doesn't matter! I prefer them poor, but alive.

— Yes mom, but dignity is essential in our lives. – I insisted to my mother, while she expelled the following words from her mouth:

— I will fight for your well-being, my son, I will not allow anyone to harm you and if your cousin wants to hit your brother again, I will use the 45 that I don't think the authorities will do anything.

—But my uncle, who is a trustee, could help us!

— No son, we are not going to ask the government for chichi. – My mother said with great resignation.

While we fixed a stone fence on the plot, my mother continued urging us to work harder.

My older brother told us:

— I want to go to Colima to study, it is a very clean and orderly city, people can sleep even with the door open and nothing happens. While I asked him:

—How are we going to pay for your studies? Answering me with great confidence:

— I'm going to live with my father's friend who is a priest. He will give me a job as a sacristan and altar boy, with that I will study and get ahead. My mother held a bar in her hands and she looked at it with concern, but at the same time she accepted the decision:

— I want you to really try hard son, if you're not a ten it doesn't matter, the grade you get is yours and with firmness and persistence follow your ideals. While I was removing the soil from a pit that my mother was digging to plant a post, I told her that Tarascan ant were coming. They are those clinging ants that prefer to die before abandoning their prey, they make furrows of thousands of members, like armies of Rome after their prey, they go one after another and pile up on their victim. They bite her and make her die of burning. Then they tear it apart piece by piece. The thought ran through me that at that moment we were being victims of jackals who see orphans and widows as easy prey. While my brother peeled a cider and the words came from him:

— In this plot, a few meters from here my father sang a song, days before he died. – I ripped off segments of the cider, that citrus fruit. While my sisters played at closing the saws saying: – shut up, here comes the devil – while the ivies serve as color in those brambles and the bumblebees fly like helicopters over the riot. – My second brother makes the fire to heat the bean tacos. The lunch hangs from a branch of a small tree. My mother takes her voice and tells us:

— In that plot next door there is a treasure, your deer uncle went to the house and sitting at the table with your father told him: - "let's go get the coins that my dad left me" - he talked about many coins, a approximately two buckets that his father took out to sunbathe on a goatskin. And he wanted to donate those coins to your father. I interrupted him saying:

— Mother and why don't we look for him?

— No son, we need a device to find it, a good metal detector. Here they use some rods to search for treasures, but I don't know how to do that witchcraft.

— Do they cost expensive?

- Yes son!

That day he finished with some grilled beans tacos with their respective cheese. We could lack money, but we could never lack corn, beans, salt and work. We could enjoy milk and cheese in the pasture season and in the dry season we saw the cows were very skinny so we could not go beyond extracting milk from them.

Getting home was glory, winning the hammock was paradise, as the bones settled and the mind was lulled.

A few meters from our house was the temple and fifty meters away was the pantheon.

In that place he took people to bury inside wooden boxes and sometimes in a mat. They did take thousands of prayers, many marigold flowers, dahlias, hollyhocks, obelisks and roses.

The ladies covered their faces with a black veil were singing praises and praying to their dead, these are the records I keep of several funerals that I have witnessed.

- Good night! A small voice was heard outside the fence of the house. It was a boy with a cup in his hand. She was going to ask if we had sugar. – "My mother tells me if they give him sugar" – I remembered that that child an hour before at school had danced in mockery that they had killed my father and I did not remain silent: – "Chilero" Do you remember that you made fun of him? that they killed my father? And that kid was ashamed and didn't tell me anything.

My mother, being a sweetheart, took the cup and filled it with sugar. Without taking into consideration that this dripping and wormy brother, at night he went to our barn to steal the corn.

My mother's tears for my father's absence are very moving, she is an example of kindness, despite the pain that cooks inside her, she is not capable of doing acts with resentment.

She told the kid: "There's no need for them to return it to me, you tell your mother that it's fine that way."

The head of that family was a first class drunk, he carried a tape recorder with regional songs, typical ranch songs and with a gallon of liquor, that diabolical liquid had already claimed many lives in that town, due to the vice of alcohol they had murdered Don Benito for stealing 50 pesos from him, they assaulted him on the road and stoned him to death. It was his son who found him, it was undoubtedly a hellish experience. The brains were scattered in the mud several meters away.

- father, father! – were the screams of a shocked son.

Families are hurt by the mistakes of beastmen who do not reason and alcohol numbs the most important organ of human beings, the brain.

Animal instinct governs the desires and passions of bestial beings who do what their animality dictates. They murder other beings simply to acquire the solvency to continue in the vice. Carboncito heard in an adult talk that a vicious person said the following:

I owe everything I am to alcohol, without it I can't be anything! Thanks to alcohol I dare to recite great poems, with ease and solemnity!

But brother! – His advisor answered. – Alcohol has taken you to a dimension that does not allow you to enjoy your family!

Yes I understand, but I can't give up alcohol! - Was the response of that drunk.

In this town a lot of drugs are produced and when the harvest comes out the farmers bring bills even to light cigarettes and wipe their butts with bills of any denomination, but that lasts a very short time; The prostitutes in the town fatten their pockets, because they make a killing with the drunks who do not know how to manage their assets; These do need an encomendero or at least a nanny to take care of them.

My relative Chavarín carries a backpack full of money, a tape recorder on his shoulder and a gun on his waist, everything looks like he's going to last a few weeks swimming in alcohol, God forbid they get hit with machetes or bullets. – My prayers ran through my mind.

When the gentlemen are doing well, they form teams and work together on loan for days, one day they work on one and the next day they work on the other and they continue in this dynamic until the work is completed.

When the women are doing well, they are not arguing, they even send each other plates of food, but when they fight they make the men angry with so many arguments and then the men are upset with each other.

The trap in the spirit.

Yesterday I had the experience of choosing my godfather and godmother for my baptism. My father gave me the choice of who would be my godparents to accompany me in the religious act that ties souls to a cross and makes them carry it all their lives like a shame that swirls in their subconscious and gives them no reason to clarify their creed. My father put me in front of some people and told me:

—Who do you want to be your godmother? Petra, cuca or chana.

— Petra! -She is the lady who was living with my father yesterday and the only one who moved me with any sympathy.

—And, who do you like for godfather?! – My father asked me. To whom I quickly answered, pointing my finger.

— Let it be "Pullo"!

- Okay son! – We agreed with my father and that's how it was.

The next day, at the temple, they put me next to a container with water and they bathed my head. I felt cool and uncomfortable because I like to bathe in the river tank, in that basin that sinks like a rose sucker and leaves all the dirt behind. In the temple the people sang praises in a secretive and annoying voice:

— hallelujah, hallelujah, hallelujah! – praises that pierce my ears for the ugly things that the old chimoleras sing, a song that, instead of redeeming the soul, makes it distance itself from those demons that pray with their mouths and kill with their hands.

They live fighting with their neighbors and when they say mass they are very pious, they even cry and shout to God.

We can see this as an excess of morality, they have double standards, which is: one thing is done in front of one's neighbor and another thing is done after him.

Very early in the morning, I was woken up by the bustle of my mother's cooking. She was preparing everything to cook a pig that would be the victim of my and my sister's baptism celebration, poor pig, they gave it a tremendous bullet in the forehead. , with that weapon that my father carries on his waist. They opened a hole with a knife under the front leg, in the chest. Blood was running everywhere, thank goodness they didn't kill it directly like the pig they killed with my aunt, the other day, they put a pig under its front leg and the pig screamed horribly, hellish screams, no one wants to kill the pig, but everyone wants to eat it.

On the ranch, people are not very insensitive, we can treat the poor animals like no one else, but it is part of our country training, harshness and insensitivity. With my slingshot I have managed to kill flying beetles and running lizards. I have not analyzed that these living beings have the right to live because I have no use in killing them. - Well, it makes me feel like a magnificent slingshot! - I see that adults practice with their weapons by putting a bullet in a small spot on a tree and I try to put the stone in the small head of a dove or at least an iguana.

Iguanas are very hard to kill, when you manage to put a stone on their head, you have to finish it off with another stone in the same place, but you have to be very precise. If they don't succeed, they run away like the devil, well I don't believe in the devil any more than in the poor people I see every day, skinny, wormy people who live damaging trees and houses with their slingshot.

I would not like to share with you in detail about the weaknesses of my people, I find gossip in bad taste, but I am going to make an exception, I will start with my grandfather, he was widowed many years ago, but he wanted to win over a widow too and now I talk about what happened:

My grandfather is a very elegant guy, with very fine features and of agricultural origin, my uncles and my father are very in love, but it is because they have a heart of a good rooster, on one occasion my grandfather said to my uncle:

—Go see the cows and check them well! To which my uncle replied happily:

- Yes Dad.

— You also check the fences and falsettos that are not coming off, take a look at the water troughs.

—As you say and order dad.

My uncle took his backpack and went into his room, he put a decent shirt and pants on it and headed to see the cows, but he found another way. My grandfather left the house a few minutes after his son's departure and his intention was to stay away from agricultural production.

- What are you doing here? – My grandfather asked when he saw his son behind a rock. With sorrow, but he answered:

— I came to see a girl. – My grandfather was a little embarrassed, but in the role of his father he complained:

— I sent you to see the cows and I found you here. – My uncle replies with a question:

- And what are you doing here? – My grandfather changed color, but he assumed his part:

— I came for the same thing.

The women left their village to go to the spring to carry water to their rooms and the lovers would wait for the moment to talk to them. They would throw a pebble into the water and they would find out that someone was checking them.

— I came to see mercy. – my grandfather replied – and you? He asked my uncle, who answered with all the sadness.

— I came to see the daughter. – At that moment the two of them discovered each other and the following days they went together to see the mother and daughter.

Another gossip that spreads around the place is that the men are very womanizers and that their wives have had infections on their tails. One woman said that her husband gave her lice, but they are not the same as the ones that run on her head. to most of my companions, they are yellow lice. Another of the gossips that can be said about the lady who sells shaved ice, her husband killed her own son because he did not obey her and shot him with a 12 gauge shotgun, that boy was left dead next to the river, in a falsetto

I could fill this book with a lot of gossip, but my objective is not to describe the evil of the people around me, but to describe how we fall into the spiritual traps of beliefs that bind us in the creed of unsupported things, make us fanatics and irrational. . On the day of my baptism I felt ashamed because my conscience was already telling me that it is neither true nor useful to pour water on people in front of them, they wet me and said a bunch of words, I didn't understand anything about them.

Going back to the adventure of my uncle and my grandfather, my uncle went to the United States to raise money to get married, but he did not return soon, she married another and when my uncle returned he found her unwell, my grandfather did not maintain the relationship with that beautiful widow.

After the baptism ceremony for my sister and me, the guests even put on their flip flops, the minor judge, my parents' friend, even stripped the jug of so much monkey he had prepared for them, the lemon tree was ragged and the sugar was almost it runs out, but the takers become brutalized to the point of peeing their pants. That, they leave themselves, they lose themselves.

The native of my town can live hungry for many days, but he does everything possible to satisfy his idolatry, they venerate their saints and swear to them as if they were truly gods, they detonate rockets that scare away dogs and cats, in this ranch The impact is greater, deer, wild boars and many other animals flee, because the noise is in bad taste and outdated. They should ban them and prevent so much damage.

A rocket caused very serious injuries to my grandmother. The rocketman missed a piece and hit my grandmother's skirt. He couldn't remove it in time and it exploded, almost knocking out a baby she was expecting. Burned and with all that ardor, she thanked God that she didn't get any worse.

Days later the rocketman's fingers got wet on one hand, a piece burst in his hand and his fingers were pulverized, but the party continues.

Many atrocities occur during these festivals, those who drink liquor then go around fighting with their neighbors, otherwise they abuse their authority by attacking their children and wife. Machismo is a very common practice in this town, the man is the one in charge while the woman has to be submissive and voiceless. Whoever is in charge has control as a whim, the orders are dictated by him, what has to be done he says.

The festivities conclude with fireworks and fireworks, some that drink until they turn black and others that actually seek meaning in the religious festival. The priest sees the party as a riot, while the children see the opportunity to play and mingle with the neighbors. and the cousins. My father at the time of my baptism is a celebrator of the word, a type of free disciple who goes and brings consciousness through religious means, they are a social religious movement that tries to be revolutionary, however, it is a form not compatible with The revolution continues to be the vain and the real wanting to merge, water and oil, wanting to merge.

Today is the last day of the patron saint's festivities and there will no longer be those noises of explosives that wake up the villagers in the early mornings and scare the dogs. I don't see the point of calling a supposed saint a patron, who was given the appointment of slavery and conquest, I know that the ignorant are business for the church and the government, the church is only control and submission, religion is totally different, it is freedom of belief, it is consciousness in the universe. People have three duties, the first is the family, the second is humanity and the third is knowledge or wisdom, in the first the ego is summarized, in the second duty the civil and human duty is combined and the third is reasoning. or duty to search for the metaphysical, for being in its entirety.

I learned this from a book I read from my father, the study of philosophy, they are books that change the individual concept of the world, but they have many vices of ideologies, ideologues enslave themselves in the traps of systems, those systems that gives comfort, pleasure, prestige and personality. In fact, there are thinkers who are born from flawed and old, obsolete and enslaving systems. Free thinkers have the value of freedom and the pleasure of saying and doing what freedom allows them, while the religious and fanatics are cloistered in the trap of the mental box. Mice fall into that box and it is no longer possible to get out of there, because when you try to cross the mental line you return for fear of violating the principles of your church.

Religious intolerance is a mistake, indifference is better, religions do not deserve contempt or hatred, much less acceptance, everything that does not liberate humans is not for them.

You will wonder why I think this way as a child, because I have heard my father speak, I have seen my community kneel in front of a priest and do the opposite of what it should be, my father's books that I have read I have done when they leave and leave my sisters in charge.

If I'm not preparing something to eat in the kitchen, I'm playing with my father's musical instruments and I'm playing with my sisters. On one occasion I prepared fried beans for my sisters, but it occurred to me to add pork rinds to them. After that greasy dish, my youngest sister almost threw them in the face. When my mother returned, she almost beat me to death with a club instead of being grateful that a six-year-old boy take care of your 3 and 2 year old sisters, it's true, my mother is very hard on me but that has no value on this ranch; She only asks that they take care of her eyes and from then on, as if they were animals, they hit the children with whatever they use their fingers for first.

If I am redundant in this pain, it is because the wound has not closed, I still remember the welts of ground blood along my legs, the other day he hit me with the horse's butt and I felt worse than an animal, at least the horse run, but if I run, my mother's voice is heard:

—If you run it will be worse for you! You have to come to sleep.

- Don't hit me mom, please! – They were my screams before receiving the blows. While my brother mocked me, saying:

- Lero, lero! – If he wasn't my brother, a shot from the mold would do me justice, but then it goes away and I love my brother very much again. While my sister yells at my mom:

- Don't hit him mommy!

—Your sister is dying because of her. – It is the justification for that brutal act of my mother. The result is invariable, the shit breaks my dignity and my honor, it is preferable that she kill me, just as she has killed my self-esteem, I prefer to follow her than to live with that pain in my chest, I have thought that violating a child in that way is commit a crime worse than leaving them in an orphanage.

I'm not going to fall into the trap, I will forgive my mother, even if we mutually don't understand each other. I will try to change my mind to another topic, I better tell you that a few moons ago, my mother sent us to look for the goats, while the storm was falling, the lightning struck the highest parts, the snakes took refuge in the caves, the ditches. They fill with water and the goats have to be deep in the rocks, up to the top of the hill where walking through the mountains not only leaves my brother and me vulnerable, but also the weeds overwhelm us, the bushes and the bushes thorn us. mites climb to our skin.

Life is so hard in the countryside that the flowers of the field are easily forgotten although their beauty is enormous. Eating a tender ear from the cornfield that left several calluses on your hands is the most delicious thing to chew when you are hungry, delighting the Green beans and egg in the morning, accompanied by warm tortillas and lemon leaf tea is sublime but that is forgotten when suffering the hard work in the fields; The nights become fleeting moments that end with dreams of fantastic beings. On one occasion I dreamed that a tiger was chasing me and I could fly like him. After discovering the reason for his chase, I saw huge gold coins in my hands. and the tiger got angry because I had those coins.

It is not possible that the time I have to rest is interrupted by terrible dreams where I am pursued by malevolent beings who want to extract my soul, that is why believing in a supreme being is successful and in the early mornings when nightmares wake me up I repeat:

— Our Father, who art in heaven... and after praying as best I can, because I don't really know the prayers of the church, I hope to hear a rooster crow to calm my fear because I heard my grandfather say:

— The rooster runs to the devil, because at the birth of Jesus a rooster crowed and the devil is afraid of the crow of the rooster.

– My fears are greater, I feel that someone is watching me, but I am under the blanket and it is impossible for me to uncover myself. I have my feet pressing the blanket and my head on the other end, if someone pulls the blanket it could break or I could go into cardiac arrest from fear. I feel the reality of nightmares and my fears are more powerful every day because I hear my cousins and brothers talk about powerful beings.

Yesterday my cousin "Agapo" was telling about witches and their relationship with owls, witches could turn into owls and go for walks at night, they also mentioned that my uncle Chavarín is a shaman who turns into an owl.

My dad sent me to my aunt Cuca's house to get oil and gave me a bottle so they could give me oil for the lighter, that's the way we light up, there is no electricity like in the town. My aunt filled the bottle for me and I returned to the house, when I was about seventy meters from the house, in a tall tree an owl sang to me at a height of three meters above my head and the fear was so great that I paralyzed. I couldn't run anymore and I fell to the floor throwing the oil and screaming in fear, I felt like I was dying, the witcher wanted to take me and I was almost in his clutches.

My father was resting in a hammock and with one jump he jumped over the fence and he went to meet me, he rubbed my head and encouraged me with his words: —Don't be afraid, son, it was nothing! -

I told him that he was a witch, that my cousin and my older brother were saying that witches turned into owls. I had fallen into the trap of psychosis and fear made me fall.

The next day my father made my cousin feel like a chicken coop, but that didn't stop me from being scared, I had nightmares and disturbing dreams for a while.

It is time to discern what I am going to do with my life, I do not have the support to be able to put together an academic record and be able to pursue a professional career. In a couple of days I am going to attend school, I will enter fourth grade and I have heard that there are boys and girls who are very intelligent. I want to go to school and be a professional, I have thought about attending marine biology school because I would not like to herd cows all my life and reinforce fences, much less do I want to live suffering the pain of physical fatigue.

My grandmother does not know how to read or write, my grandfather learned as an adult, he does not know more than the basics, therefore, they have no affection for academic training, my grandfather told my mother that it was not necessary for us to study, that He would teach us to work hard and with that we would earn our daily bread. My father always insisted to my mother that we should study to be someone in life.

I wonder if those who don't study are anyone in life? I know that they are, but they are not enough to offer development for the country, progress is there, in the peasant improving his way of production, the rancher improving his way of farming and the worker being able to produce his own companies, but not to remain in that regression of doing the same thing every generation, producing in a traditional way and without evolving.

—How was my brother? – My mom asked.

- Okay mom! – I showed him my hands and he saw my bleeding blisters.

—Come my child, I'm going to check you for ticks! – My mother started looking behind my ears and in my armpits, she put cempaxúchitl on my welts and after resting for a while, that day, she bathed me in the basin with her hand. My grandfather was talking to my mother:

—Your children do know how to work, they just lack speed. – my grandfather said with great confidence.

- Yes, they know, dad! His father taught them. – My mother answered.

— In a few days they will be given the land that you paid to your brother and they will be able to plant sorghum, corn and grass for their cows.

- Yes Dad! My mother answered.

—The next day will be Sunday and we are going to go greet my uncles, cousins and get to know the town.

Like almost all towns there was an up and down, my grandfather was located at the top. In the ejidal house a record player was playing, it was the jilguerillas from Michoacán who were repeating a song at full volume: "go paloma and tell him", my grandfather gets passionate stimulated by some beer, then the ejidatarios arrive to dance.

Through a window I start to see how the old people dance, they do very complicated country steps. My grandfather dances with his sister and they achieve harmony in their dance, I like to see his movements. I have started to meet my cousins, nice people.

Everything indicates that the health of the social being depends on each person, I feel good within this circle of agrarian people, although the pain of leaving my father behind, regardless of the state he is in, is my honor and my dignity. that is hurt. I keep thinking about revenge and taking back my father's lands that were taken from us. I know that I am a child to fall into the trap of hatred and revenge, but I remember what they did with my father and I would like to do that with all of them. loved ones and my uncles to return the favors they did with my family and make them pay for their disloyalty to my father.

I ask the creative being to heal me from this anger that invaded my being, but I cannot overcome it, however, I know that in this town I will heal and I will be able to lift my fight. The fight for life and for the health of my being, to grow.

The tiger trap.

In that place there are many tigers, but one in particular is the Vallejo tiger, that tiger is cunning and very aggressive, but there is a tiger hunter who is just as evil, that is my uncle, the one who has generated aggression in the family . The Vallejo tiger swallows the cows, devours them and turns them into nothing, that tiger seems to have two legs, which carries the ruminants with a lasso to its corral.

My uncle is very brave and at night he goes up to the mountain range and tries to hunt the tigers so that they stop harming the cattle, but the two devourers also hunt deer. On that occasion, one dark night in December, he took his maca, his backpack and his shotgun. In the half-mochado sack bag he carried inside "oko" for "the salsaguates" and ticks, his tobacco for leafy cigars. and his lunch, some shots from a shotgun and an executioner inside his case to butcher the unfortunate deer.

He mounts the road and with a shotgun on his shoulder he flies through the air, heading towards the hill, arriving at the point chosen as suitable for hunting, he ties his mace from one end to the other between the high branches of a tree and waits for a prey to fall to his side. his aim, in that place there is a spring of water and paths from all sides that lead to that source of clean water, purified by the passage through the bowels of the earth. The thread runs for several meters and then gets lost in the sand.

The mosquitoes begin to bother, especially those insects called borers, they eat the blood through their ducts that they bury in the skin, they suck the blood and then they are no longer able to fly. They look like Mexican politicians, they bloat themselves and then they want to hide their bellies, but they are so heavy that they can't even run, that is, they can't hide their hunger.

My uncle uses his cigarettes, the smoke makes the mosquitoes leave and not land on the target. Around three in the morning, a deer is heard approaching to drink water and accurate pellets come out of the barrel of that shotgun and hit the deer's rump, it jumps and falls very close to the water, as it goes down. The hunter hears a new noise, but of a different nature. The footprints are with claws and evil, it is the vallejo tiger that is going to beat the hunter's prey, he shines the light in the feline's eyes and sees that ferocity in them. He tries to shoot him, but his gun jams and he escapes with his prey.

Carboncito crosses the hill with his brother in search of the cows that they took to graze on the hill, they do not find the best heifer, the whereabouts of this special specimen of the Swiss Indo-Brazil cross is unknown, a specimen that does not deserve to have a different purpose other than reproduction, so it will be used to give birth to many calves. But it does not appear. The tiger took her, there is a tiger that operates in this mountain range and causes damage to local ranchers, apparently that tiger has two legs. Yes, a human-shaped animal will one day fall and be hunted like a mad dog.

I feel committed to supporting my mother and my siblings, but I am just a child, at eleven years old I cannot do much more than try to do adult jobs in the fields, those jobs are very hard, because the tools They are not advanced and it is done in an artisanal way, from sowing with coa to harvesting with piscalón, fencing the plots with wire and fumigating the cows with a sprayer. The pastures are a lot of work for my brothers and my mother, since we have to collect "marquerón" plants, a special type of cane for cattle pastures. That is why it makes me very angry that there are people who steal other people's things, especially when they steal from orphans and a widow, it is the worst. The heifer was lost and someone took it from the place and we know that it is the Vallejo tiger, that animal that leaves no trace.

Palapa buyers have arrived at the ranch, they are people who come from Puerto Vallarta, Nuevo Vallarta and other tourist places, in these spaces life is luxurious, I could never manage to eat a plate of food in a restaurant where 300 grams of meat of beef costs half a cow of mine, if not more. The buyers take the palapa for two pesos already cut and placed in a place where they can take it in their trucks, but it is difficult to cut them and, above all, to drag them to the edge of the gap, like donkeys my brothers and I pull, we manage to count two thousand palapas, that money is going to be a huge help for my mother who earns very little money as a rural health assistant. I remember well when she left us to go take the paramedic course in the city of San Blas, where she was taught a lot and she was of great use to the people of the ranch.

Today at school I sang to the girls, I sing to them with all my heart, the songs hurt me when I sing them and I think I'm going to be a singer like my father, the one who sang his songs on the back of his horse and while he was tilling the land , I like the joy of songs, I like the therapy of singing to release all the stress and illnesses of the soul. He who sings healthy songs reaches the universe and even the great creator of the universe is happy to hear them. The teacher has chosen me to sing at the Mother's Day festival and I have rehearsed in the middle of the field and surrounded by all the students, I have been embarrassed to sing and stage fright, I think it is difficult to sing in public, especially without be prepared as a singer.

The days have passed and the date of May 10 has arrived, a day that moves all Mexicans, Mother's Day, and it happened to me in front of many women and men of various ages, including my mother and some aunts, my aunt Chuy started crying when she heard me sing, the song of the four candles was played in that ranch and between nerves my voice came out acceptable, as the song should not come out if I sing it to the four winds with all the vigor of a professional singer. The girl I like is here in the audience and she is the one who motivates me to sing with greater strength and dedication, my mother I don't even know where she is, but the girl who makes me blush is next to her mother and looks at me carefully, However, she doesn't know what I like, I have told another girl if she wants to be my girlfriend through a little letter.

On weekends we get together with my cousins in the bullring, where we ride the calves to try our luck and awaken the adrenaline, of being on the back of a beast, although we are children we are very daring and the Luck can change if a ruminant knocks us to the ground. On March 21, spring is celebrated and they do jaripeo dancing, the bullring is filled with people, bulls and music, with banda rhythms, people drink beers and dance, the riders prepare to ride a bull, while the girls get rid of fear when seeing the groom prepare the lassos to mount the animal. The charros ride their horses, with soguillas in hand, ready to lasso the bull after it is mounted.

On March 21, my classmate in primary school, made a bet with his brother, that he had to endure 5 objections to a bull, which, he noticed in turns, endured five and on the sixth, the bull fainted and fell silent with the rider. on his back, the editor hit his head and was unconscious. He was rushed to Puerto Vallarta where he died while in the hospital. That brother felt like he was dying. He had bet him a trousseau if he would keep it, everything that a rancher wears at a party, boots, socks, pants, pants, shirt, woven belt and hat.

At the funeral they gave us coffee and cinnamon with picket, I put some in my coffee, as a child alcohol became present in my life and I fell into the trap of the enervating. I Marie a little. But it was not the first time I tried it, on one occasion my father took a bottle home and hung it on a beam and due to political activities he would leave the house for days. My brothers and I took alcohol and poured water into it, in the end it was almost pure water, when my father came back, he made himself a coffee in the morning and went to put alcohol in it, he tried his coffee and it didn't taste like a picket at all, he called to his children and made them confess the facts, to which my brother Mayos said, my cousin Agapo told us to make some monkeys with lemon and sugar, then we didn't know what to do to cover the gap and we poured water into the bottle. Enraged, my father called Agapo and put him as a chicken stick. But since then I liked the effect of alcohol, although I have heard that it does a lot of harm to people by becoming a vice.

When people die, they leave a void in the beings who love them. Those who do not have a mourner do so because their life was not important to anyone. That companion left and was needed in the living room. His excessive courage and the insolence of his brother killed him. brother; It reminds me of my father who left a void in me, in my family and in the community.

On this ranch life seems very boring in ordinary time, if it weren't for playing soccer with my cousins and cousins, life on this ranch would not be attractive at all. In the challenges, all the kids get together to kick the ball and we make a shout, the leader is my cousin Yati, she leads all the people, she is a born leader and very kind, we all love her and respect her because she puts order in our lives. children's relationships. My aunt María, her mother, is a very big and strong woman, she is very hard-working and above all she is a very good person, she takes care of my sisters and I as if we were hers, she shelters us with her love and we believe that she is a woman sent from god

In the secondary school, which is next to the soccer field, there are machines that tell everything, I think you ask them and they tell you everything you want to know, they are high-tech machines that connect them to the light and they ask you questions , they call them computer. I want to learn how to use one but there are none for my school, only high school students use those machines. Next door is the street to my house, the adobe house that has cement tiles is where we live with my mother and my brothers, in the lower part of the land and on the slope we have banana plants, in the upper part the nances abound and mango petacón, some avocados and a few meters away is the bullpen where we do our illegal children's jaripeadas.

In the northern part of the ranch, live my uncles Panchito and Joselito, two bachelors who did not get married because the women dress and fit, they eat daily and that is why they did not get married, they like alcohol and repeat the records of the goldfinches many times. , a diet of rural women, of Michoacan origin, who sing very beautiful songs. Life in a small town is special, everyone knows your defects and never recognizes your virtues, they dedicate themselves to analyzing your life and leave their own aside. They give their opinion on what you have to do and how you have to do it, but they don't do their homework. Life in society is complicated because they always try to bombard you with predetermined patterns of behavior and set the tone for you to behave the way they want you to, but it is not always the best, we have to question everything and be critical, but that is not Society likes generations to think and stop reproducing their predetermined forms of behavior. It is not bad as long as the rules and the law are not violated.

In that corner of the western Sierra Madre there are some small houses in the fortune of that geographical point where the plain of the river and the shore of the mountain meet, there in that ranch lived little charcoal, the boy who sang to the girls of the primary school and he sang to the waves of air that carried his voice in the crop fields, in the grasslands of the hills, he sang when he was afraid, when he was happy, when he remembered a good song he heard on the radio or on the voice of his father.

In the primary school, everything was prepared for graduation, the ceremony teacher gave instructions to the students who would leave that premises to go to try a higher grade in secondary school, Charcoal practiced the waltz with two huge girls who, despite being the largest tallest in his group, his two companions were taller.

Little coal from the bottom of my heart, I wish you well where you are going!

Thank you very much teacher. I am going to travel to the cleanest and safest city in the country.

I hope that you achieve your dreams and that the light reaches you so that you can be a useful citizen. The countryside is dignified and is the basis of our economy, because, just as primary school is the basis of secondary school, the countryside is the basis of industry and the economy. I sincerely wish that you achieve your goals, that everything is prosperous and abundant.

Thank you very much teacher!

The city trap.

Carboncito, after the vacation after his graduation, prepared to travel to the city where he would continue his studies. One day in the morning a type of bus that looks like a skeleton of a bus got on the "bullfight", like chairs and without bus walls, everything in free dust, you travel from the ranch to the next town, through the gap and the potholes. They make the poor boy jump, who is thoughtful with his backpack and his luck tightly pressed. After so many potholes and puddles they reach San Juan debajo, a town that looks like a swamp with so many mudflats and puddles.

He gets off the skeletal truck and heads to the combis, small hot vehicles that go back and forth from San Juan to Vallarta, in that charcoal little place he boards a bus that carries "gringos" heading to Manzanillo. The boarding was very strange, stunned by ignorance and little or no experience in traveling alone, the boy arrived at the central station where he asked the ticket seller for a truck heading to the port near the south, she took him by the hand to the door of the truck and told the driver to unload it in Manzanillo, so he did. But they didn't charge him anything, from Manzanillo to Colima they charged him 17 pesos, he reserved an amount of money that would end up buying new pants. Carboncito boarded a taxi that charged him ten pesos to take him to the temple where his brother and the priest were waiting for him.

Carboncito arrives at the spirit trap, in that enormous construction many voices were enclosed that could be heard in the silence of the night, laments, screams of pain, energies flying as if desperate and that child was exposed to all that rain of negativities. When people go to a temple, they release their bad energies and become trapped in the place where they navigate until they find a new recipient.

God is sold as a commodity and from that moment on the great creator is offensive. The priest talks about being good people, doing good and elevating our goodness above all by having in front of him the collection of offerings or alms. The priests talk to you about being a good husband, father, good mother or good person and it is a bottomless invitation, well, they have never helped the people to have better living conditions, to improve their educational level, to increase their dedication to our country. and increase love between humans. The priest tells the public in his speech, but it is empty and without example. The priest promotes morality and carries moral vices that tear his habits.

Little Charcoal felt loneliness, his throat fell silent and he no longer sang, while the church rang in praise, Little Charcoal missed his cows and walking through the fields, playing with vines, riding calves and climbing his beasts. The church, an inquisitive moralistic institution that punishes human behavior with morbidity and evil, without giving it the opportunity to respond or defend itself, is an empire of jackals that numb the will of people and make them beasts of work, souls without growth or construction of personality, the church does the complete opposite of that revolutionary and great rebel named Jesus, a human martyr who has made him a business and elevated him to God so that his ideals are neither reasonable nor achievable by humans, but remain in the walls of the temple, Jesus did not seek the formation of sedentary and dogmatic churches that instead of preaching by example preach hollow, bottomless speeches, however the universal principles are forever and throughout the universe, although the practitioners are seen as fools and outside the system, a social mode that attacks humanity, the great creator and creation itself because it is considered a trap built from deep human evil, I am referring to the construction of the capitalist system inherited from the slave and feudalist regime, it is a human trap in which we find ourselves trapped without being able to break that human curse.

Jesus came to break with that human foolishness, being a disciple of universal principles and philosophical science, especially morality, this great man appeared as a great at the level of great thinkers of Egypt and Greece, same thoughts that follow Subject to the compass and the rule for the good of humanity, it is about combating the vices of humanity, these that sicken the soul and hurt the divine creation and offend its great creator.

In the temple, charcoal knew evil due to the ignorance of those who practice it and due to the intention of those who have a sick soul. From there he could see people with physical vices that harm their bodies, traps that are difficult to combat because they take root in the human mind and if this false need is not satisfied, the addict continues in the struggle to achieve satisfaction, the vices degrade the person. person and increase large profits for the owners of the distributors, I am not referring only to drugs, but to legal merchandise that generates a human dependency that, if this innovation or fashion is not satisfied, one suffers to the point of losing a healthy esteem and integral, real and essential self-conceptualization of the person.

Carboncito met a plump woman whose aroma was fresh, pleasant, very tasty and gave the impression of excessive care of her person, from her fingers hung nails longer than the tigers in "Fortuna", she got out of a very nice car, Her face was flirtatious and very bright, the beautiful woman exchanged a few words with charcoal asking him for the location of the priest and in a contemptuous manner looked up and down the neighborhood with charcoal, giving him little attention due to his humble appearance and his ranch huaraches. The woman is in that trap called social division where they say that some are above and others are below, the division of the world into social classes is a trap that does not leave humans free, it chains them to act in a way that does not harm their status and its comfort, when humans are free they leave those chains that bind their thoughts and souls and live their freedom fully.

Freedom is nothing more than that difficult quality of not being tied to any vice, to any prejudice to any human that limits its free development, free thought, that is why religions are for weak humans who need an ideology. to control their evil and their lack of principles and values. Free humans do not concern themselves with religions, they only concern themselves with being governed by that conglomerate of moral precepts that fill their spirit to act for the good of humanity and the supreme being creator of the universe. Human religions undermine freedom and lead humans to a vice of behavior where they repeat and repeat the same vice, its evil. Religion as a religious institution is necessary to lull the weak to prevent them from thinking and aspiring to freedom. It is a very effective trap that entangles the spirit and truncates its free development. If free men have religiosity, it is that encounter with the great creator through his disposition in meditation and gratitude for everything that exists. Religion is that choice of that participation of the great architect of the universe and the wonderful work of him, the universe.

Carboncito continued cleaning the temple while doing his theological reasoning, the pain in his back occurred due to overwork, at twelve years old he was doing the work of an adult, the pay was a roof, food, clothing, money for school , is the consequence of his father having died from the bullets of capitalism.

Little Charcoal got up every morning to go to school and learn the instructions of the system, where humans are forced to learn the same thing and in the same way, so that their behavior is simultaneous: physically produce, survive and devour when possible. You are not educated to be conscious, in fact, you are not educated, you are educated to be an employee and servant of the system, you are not educated to think and reason, that does not serve the system because a world of thinking people would demand a just state and, that's not business.

Carboncito learned to get on the bus in the morning and travel to his school, the bus has the capacity for 38 people and there are about fifty, people are standing and packed together like sardines, the students in the morning have faces like horses. scolded and the ladies look beautiful just bathed, with their hair combed half wet, their freshness is contagious, on those cool mornings people are passive; nothing to do with the departure of the students at noon, the students come euphoric and their behavior is more active and playful, the boys are talking loudly, joking and the midday heat is oppressive. Carboncito has barely learned to travel from the temple in which he serves as an employee to school and vice versa. The first time, he got lost and the truck driver was very rude, denying him information and how to get back to his house. After abandoning the truck, Carboncito was lucky to find a person who told him how to get to the temple. .

When Charcoal felt sad he would start dancing because moving his body relieves stress and singing feeds his soul. Charcoal felt imprisoned in that world where he still could not adapt, but there was something he liked about the city, the possibility to get ahead, to obtain preparation to serve humanity and fulfill its ideals. When his father was alive, he told him that his goal in childhood and youth is to prepare for maturity, this has to be through academic preparation, that is, elevating the spirit, cultivating the mind to be able to be a better person and above all for the love of The humanity. The profession is for the service of humanity and with it come benefits for its performance, the fruits of the tree you grow are payment for the effort made.

On the ranch we could not have access to education, the peasants do not have access to education or access to universities, this is believed by apathetic people without a comprehensive vision. The peasants do have access to ideas, the peasants and workers have to improve their ideas of production, but above all of organization, in them lies the discord and harmony in the system, the tertiaries and gray men rob them of that possibility of have progressive and prosperous development. Humans, regardless of the job or profession they perform, have the duty to cultivate their spirit in a secular, scientific and loving way. In other words, every human being must have the right to education and to build their being attached to universal principles and away from prejudices, taboos, dogmas, conservatism and, above all, fanaticism.

Whoever has fanaticism does not have the ability to live free and freedom is a gift from the great architect of the universe, whoever does not have freedom of thought, does not have the faculty of reasoning and whoever does not reason does not practice freedom, that is why we have a sick system, where many people die because they do not have freedom, many people live in hell of mental illness, because they do not have freedom, mental freedom. That freedom that is the basis of happiness, the experiences or chains condemn humans to live unhappily and that is business for the gray men, those who generate false needs in you so that you live addicted to their offers, those are traps that carboncito has discovered, which he read in a book by a rebellious philosopher who was a precursor of the Mexican revolution.

Carboncito visits the zoo and sees the animals in their cages, he considers that they are a portrait of himself, he remembers the coyotes that were roaming the chickens, haughty and cunning, behind those steel bars, they look sad, oppressed and not They have their spirit free, this is how humans live in cities, locked up and worrying about monetary accounts, they also live taking care of the backs of even those closest to them, harmony does not reign in human beings who live in constant desire for money . Happy are the men and women who fight to build themselves day by day and expect from that construction, better human beings who live the universal values and principles of fraternity, freedom, truth and, above all, the practice of desirable behavior.

Those letters will not bring anything good to charcoal, rebellion has no place in a system where one governs with lies, one is educated with falsehood and mediocrity, dogmas are indoctrinated without room for reason, creeds act as shock absorbers that try to soften beasts so that they do no harm, but they do business with divinity and fanaticism. Religions are neither good nor bad, they are not necessary for humanity of reason, but they are necessary for beings without reason.

Carboncito tries to understand why humans are divided into various sectors, Carboncito has had to live in extreme poverty, in which tortillas with salt are the delicacy of a child who lacks the slightest thing to live and no one turns to look. its lack and its pain; In that place of origin they did not celebrate the holidays with banquets on the mahogany table, with silver cutlery and unlike this rich neighborhood where the ten-room house for three or four people is so small for the size of the solitude and emptiness. who live.

In its origin, work brought about what was necessary to live, you work on planting and harvesting products to eat, the producer only has one option, to produce and live a rustic life and without roughing up the harshness of his being, he is a being. that suits the system, a poor, conformist being without ideals seen with the light of reason.

In that moment of seeing the animals locked in their cages, it brought to him in charcoal the memories of seeing those eagles fly through the air, firm, fast, tenacious, brave and above all precise, when he was working with his father, he was a peasant man. , told him that eagles were impressive beings, that at thousands of meters high they were capable of seeing a tiny mouse and hunting it quickly. In that charcoal bean field he managed to see an eagle that dropped from a dive and almost touched the ground. It took flight again with something in its legs, a golden eagle could reach the size of an adult person and lift a small deer. In that zoo there were eagles, sad and without the breath of life, it was not possible to see them that way, a true sadness.

In that zoo the animals appear like humans cornered in their prison cells where they can leave at any time, be in a stadium with thousands and they continue to be prisoners, prisoners of those chains that bind their soul and cloud their spirit, to their body numbs it and makes them slaves to vices, vices that present themselves in the form of progress, in superfluous needs that enslave consumerism and vanity. That's why Carboncito says that the world is governed by drugs that act as painkillers. We have as the first drug the lie or fallacy used by churches and politicians, as the philosopher said: "the opium of the people", next we have physical drugs, legal and illegal pharmaceutical business, these elevate empires and degenerate humanity . Consumerism is a vice that maintains capitalism in its final stage, where the means of communication and transportation shorten the distance and act as a link in supply and demand, link and delivery.

That is why technology maintains a constant production of products with a limited duration, perishable systems in a certain time that makes the consumer constantly replace them and creates the need to have them and be at the forefront. Whoever is not up to date believes that he is not of our time, however, making a deep analysis of the results of technological advances, the use of mind control substances, ecclesiastical and governmental alienation, as well as the social system in which We live and realize that man has stopped being "a wolf of man" and has become a devourer of the planet, with the desire to satisfy the supply and demand of excessive consumers. The industry is in a constant revolution of products and a accelerated production and consumption of renewable and non-renewable resources.

In that zoo, in the most hidden corner there is a group of Mexican wolves, they walk and walk like prisoners in the fifth prison, their dynamics have been broken, the alpha coyote feels like the human who was stripped of his land to be taken away to the city, where he has spent his body buying houses for the rich, while he cannot afford to build a hut.

The wolf and the man have lost their identity and have been involved in superstitions and harm, their memory has been erased and the most sacred thing has been stolen from them, their spirit, that is, the creative and constructive word, the one that must be defended before the universe, The sacred word is the one that emanates from the soul and defends itself with the body and spirit, the word is the essence of things, reason and reasonableness arise from it; reason as a human faculty and reasonableness as the practice or resolution of moral principles.

There are humans who still fight for birthright like animals, since the world gives rise to free human beings with good morals, not slaves or masters, these vices are derived from the bad practices of humans of stripping others of their dignity and making them servants, arises from the economic form of social organization, that is, from the social mode.

The trap that Carboncito lives in at this moment when he sees the animals in prison in that zoo is the trap of anguish, his being is filled with fear because he is being stripped of his origin and his environment as a peasant, by decision of his parents. He has to comply with his father's order to study and "be someone in life." The donkey locked in its nature and its luck makes it appear to the public as just that, a donkey, it is for this reason that we have the moral obligation to study, to be better every day, to build ourselves at all times, but that construction has an end and It has guidelines, the last are the moral principles and the end is love for humanity, with this the duty is fulfilled for oneself, for one's peers and for the great creator.

Carboncito rents a boat where the water supports it between slats and green pasture, that dirt kills breathing and he believes that the fish that live in that filth are like humans who breathe all the waste from the machines, they dirty his body and they take away health. His lungs become dirty with the particles that enter their interior, these run through his body and then cause fatal damage, including the degeneration of cells.

The pleasure trap.

The day of visiting the zoo concludes with a reflection where Charcoal realizes that the human tries to represent with these spaces and the animals his previous origin, where he lived among nature, the dangers were natural. Nowadays, the dangers are silent, secret, intentional and very well remunerated monetarily speaking. Let's go there, it is dangerous to have little fight against vices because they divert us from our divine, natural and human mission, making us captive to fixations, to vices.

Carboncito walks through the streets of that clean and attractive city, where there are shops selling merchandise of all kinds, but the most monumental is a basilica in which the counters sell miracles and relief for the soul, these merchandise cannot be seen. , but they are bought. Humans walk like ants everywhere and buy everything you offer them, even if they don't use it or it kills them little by little. The human being has exceeded his body, they feed him everything that harms him and then when he is sick they want to cure him, when in reality the economic system makes him sick with contaminated products and, above all, useless products.

Genetic alteration is a danger in the hands of evil people, they are generating physically improved beings and products with shorter production times, products that alter our entire body. Substances are applied in production that alter the human central nervous system and keep it dependent and numb. It is also intended to make humans genetically suitable for the system, who are classified into beings by specific categories and objectives, by status and by production roles, in a classified way the owners of the world, the servants with completely defined characteristics, improving their appearance and abilities. attitudes and aptitudes. At a moment in the history of humanity, humans will find themselves connected to technology, improved in their genetics and in coexistence with artificial intelligence.

You will see from afar the times where they used substances to make many happy and control the behavior of many others, as well as the use of drugs to accumulate tons of dollars for empires, all of that will remain in history, that is if we do not end the planet. or a power madman decides to launch viruses to exterminate humanity, as they have been experimenting with COVID and other viruses of human extermination will come.

Man falls into the trap of protagonism, of standing out from others, accumulating figures of money that are not usufructuary, out of vanity and madness of power, stealing from other beings the surplus value of their work, these sick vicious beings have no limit or codification morality based on love and duty.

Carboncito arrives home for tempere and asks his tutor about freedom and he gives him a philosophical briefing on this very complex concept, Carboncito understood that freedom is the human quality of exercising his duties and rights in an emancipated way, rational and reasonable, attached to ethics and morality, but, above all, attached to respect for the other, for the other and for oneself. Priests always adapt all universal philosophy to their version of religion, churches are that usurpation of ideas for the benefit of their institution.

In the history of humanity, millions of behaviors have been repeated and what is truly valuable has been omitted, ideas, essences, non-profit coding, behaviors free of prejudices and ideological tendencies, the human mind is easy to become contaminated because There is no independence or autonomy in the act of thinking, exercising or executing ideas and acting in a social environment, we are subject to a system made up of individuals, whoever does not act attached to that system is marginalized, discarded, discriminated against, imprisoned , murdered, flogged and many other things; As an example we have Socrates, who was forced to drink hemlock after being imprisoned and put on trial. We can also cite as a great example Jesus of Nazareth, a free man with good morals, he prepared himself and raised his spirit in an impressive way, because he was a rebel for his time and for the government systems, he was murdered and then the same people who They murder him, God does it.

The trap of believing in what everyone believes is a capture of the will and makes you a being of the masses and loyal to the system, regardless of where you go, you enter a system that limits your freedom, not by telling you this I incite you to violence or to do acts that would steal your goodness and your physical freedom, what makes us free is our central system and the capacity for rationing, but above all our actions governed by the love of humanity make us free.

Carboncito feels cornered and with few opportunities, his brother begins to harass him and point out:

Father, my charcoal brother doesn't clean the temple well! – pointed out the brother.

Is he true son?! asked the priest.

Father, I try to clean everything well, besides, I had never mopped, cleaned, dusted or tidied! At the ranch we have no floor, we have no benches, no street, and no flower vases. I do what I can. – Carboncito refuted.

Son, we must have everything clean, here old high-born pompous ladies come and then they start complaining, you can improve the cleanliness!

Yes father, I will do it, but my brother must pay me well, he receives the money and he gives me what he wants in payment per week!

Well, put a price on cleanliness! – said the priest.

I have asked my brother for 30 pesos a day and he gives me 15 pesos! He says it's a lot of money for me, then he enjoys the week's pay with his friends. – Carboncito accused.

"I'm going to pay you 20 pesos a week," said the older brother.

that's better! – said the priest.

Well, I want a little more, -said Charcoal- because the temple is huge and at twelve years old I get very tired shaking, sweeping, mopping and arranging for mass.

that's OK! – said the priest – we all get tired and we have to give more effort.

Life is a give and take, when there is no balance in one of the two elements, injustices are generated and injustice breaks freedom - Carboncito's thoughts began - respect and many qualities of human life. My brother builds a house while I do his work, with the promise that as long as her mother lives, that house will be hers, but over time people change their minds.

Never fall into the trap of giving and taking, my grandfather said that he who gives and takes with the devil gets even, humans are very changeable because they lack values, that is why they use instruments to enforce their word, their rights. , agreements and commitments. This is how documents are used that force people to keep their word. Thus, the word has ceased to be valid, the essence of things ceases to be valid because material interests overlap, leaving the spiritual essences in the background, from the word value arises, the symbol arises, the symbol represents the thing and The essence is extracted from the thing, it is a cycle. However, mythologies say that everything arises from the word and it is the spiral-shaped word that gives rise to everything that exists.

Today, little charcoal has found out that everything in the world is full of traps, the trap that is most enjoyed is that of pleasure, it shelters you in sweetness, it boasts of softness and satisfaction, but pleasure never has an end. happy, so the key to vices is pleasure. In the world there is an elite that lives from pleasure, because life does not give them pleasure, so they become dependent on pleasure to hide their blockage from reality, which reality? To the reality of ideals and virtue. Gray humans become addicted to money and their money buys them pleasure, while they distance themselves from the essence of life, which consists of interpreting the world freely and without chains of deviant values, especially the value of one's own life and of others.

The trap of pain is common among the poor, believing that everything has to be endured, poverty and lack of value, the poor believe they are victims, and always assume they are victims because a chain has been placed on them, that is, a trap to set. the other cheek when they slap him and lower his gaze, that is an aberration and a crime, the human should never lower his gaze before a mortal and even less his knee, preferable to crawl in the blood than to live with the yoke of a powerful one. The poor man has been taught with that trap called paternalistic education, where they tell him that he has to be a very good employee and so much so that Charcoal gets angry when they force him to put on a uniform for school, they uniform him like in the factory, they uniform him To look like the others in their student union, they educate them to be obedient and receive instructions effectively.

They do not educate us to be free, it is one of the carbon badges, they instruct us to be useful during the time of productivity and then they throw us away like old machines, they send us to our home, if we managed to obtain one, so that in that space Invest your savings in medicines, trying to maintain life for an extra time. In the end he dies because he got used to being in the cage like the dove and doesn't know how to fly.

Pleasure is that gift that nature gave us to enjoy it with balance, if it exceeds it we become hedonists, if we do not enjoy it we become moralists, pleasure is a feeling that occurs in some occasions and situations in a way spontaneous, natural and free but the detail is in what generates such pleasure and the fixation we have on it. We find the enervating perfume of flowers that drives the hummingbird crazy with pleasure, it is its essence to live off of it, just as it generates inexplicable pleasure for man to contemplate the firmament or perceive a soft smile, the pleasure generated by the search for truth is like Swimming in a rose garden in search of a carnation, the truth is not pleasant, only the search for it. He who does not seek it is renouncing his divine essence and clings to being an instinctive being and tries to survive in a world that does not belong to him. The key to pleasure is balance, without it we incur extremism and the extremes go against the right middle, it is not staying in mediocrity, no. It is knowing how to move on the scales and obtain balance.

Here in the temple I manage to see people sick in their soul, others sick in their emotions and others even more sick in their body due to the previous two, all because there is no balance. You renounce life with happiness to live with pleasure, the pleasure of bringing the best car and not walking, the pleasure of buying the best flavors and giving up nutrients, the pleasure of meeting real people to interact with hypocrites, you accept the pleasure of drink the best wine in front of those who expect your defeat. Real people enjoy the pleasure of being able to get closer to transparent spirits and souls, they enjoy walking and hugging a tree contemplating the great creation, instead of occupying that bench with red or gold cushions in the temple, a place where the divine is monetized. Pleasure is that sweet trap that makes humans fall in love, but without it, the world would be different.

The Sanity Trap.

Carboncito wondered if humans can be crazy and pretend to be sane, or sane and remain among many sane people who are actually crazy. In truth, the problem is knowing if we are sane or crazy and follow patterns of behavior by imitation and without reason. Sanity is the trap that makes humans live life according to what is established by the order of behavior. According to the pre-established patterns of behavior for human beings according to the systematic social structure.

Human behavior is attached to common patterns of behavior, so much so that there are professionals in the treatment of atypical behaviors or behaviors outside the norms, uses and customs. In reality, the system makes us according to its needs, that is, we are like trees that are born in the forest and the needs move us towards their satisfaction, that is how we grow straight, crooked or tilted if we grow. The tree dies if the system does not allow it to grow and remains, as my grandfather says: "stunted", stunted and its fruits are vain, then we have very wise beings because they break the bars of the trap and decide to grow despite every obstacle. and they build their being, they make it clear of those vices and roughness that make it a sick tree. This can be achieved with the help of philosophy, morality and, above all, the ideals that place human beings in front of that true pleasure of loving their neighbor. Christ said: love your neighbor as yourself, we cannot directly love each sick person who walks through the world, we must love our actions and take care of them so that they do not harm any being in the world, that our love transcends the great creation of the almighty and that our conduct is free from evil. The duties for our mother nature must be with that love for what is intrinsic to her and therefore the interpretation of her will be with that light that generates reason and love.

The health of the individual is found in the balance or fair medium, in the limit or margin that he or she exercises with others, with due respect for the rights and duties of others, the other and the other.

The flow of ideas within the brain is subject to the experiences, experience and nature of the person; their mental condition gives them the possibility of being able to plot ideas and generate a resolution on the phenomenon or problem to be solved. The problem that humans have is that they educate us not to think until we are adults, however, the best age to think is when we are children, because the capacity for wonder is very sensitive and above all the need to understand and interpret the world is lush.

Children like charcoal get entangled in understanding the world and can generate particular ideas about things, for example: when charcoal's father took him to the sea, he asked his father, Dad, where does the sea end? The answers were too high to understand, Charcoal believed that the world was flat like a table and the sea ended in a waterfall, the water volatilized when it fell into the void and returned in the form of a storm. In ancient times people believed that the world was flat, then there was a stir against those who said that the planet was round, that the sun did not rotate, but that the earth was the one that, when moving, thinking differently can cost us even life, but really think.

The human being is very zealous in defending what is finished, he opposes the new, then he accepts it and then something new arises, different from the previous one and the mind once again has conflict and while doing the adaptation process it generates impetus against the discoverer of something new. So we cannot say that humans are healthy beings, because they are not free from prejudices, taboos, conservative ideas and petty ways of screwing others.

The trap in judgment is the distortion of reality and ignorance, ignorance is a trap that the system has generated to keep human beings stupid, and thus, have control of their minds. If an organ is not used it atrophies, that is why the brain is not used, so that the owners of the world can control people. They give them false senses of freedom to keep them busy defending that falsehood. They motivate them to defend anything and they remain embraced by that false ideal. Also the owners of money trick humans into not using their heart, they tell them that we only have 5 senses when in reality we have more receptors. The heart is a complement to the human, the entity is made up of three main elements: the body that transports the spirit and the soul that comes from divine creation, the first is the material medium that allows us to carry out actions in this world, It allows us to interact materially with the environment, but the soul is that human phase that connects us and makes us participate as an integration of the supreme being and from these arises the spirit, the latter is the result of physical and spiritual interaction, the spirit is the product of The existence of the individual is the shelter and result of their actions, that is why we have beings with a magnificent spirit, because their soul and body are in balance and above all regulated by universal principles, tending to honor their creator.

The trap is not allowing you to discover your spirituality, not to achieve balance with your body and your mind, thus, we are tripartite beings, composed with a mathematical measurement, governed by energy and subject to matter, when our soul and flies to the great light, our body remains integrated into matter and our spirit remains in the samples of facts, this is how the spirit of a painter remains in his works, that of the bricklayer remains in his work, that of the writer in his letters and so on infinitely.

That is why the trap of sanity is attached to the slavery of ideas and the illness of the body, humans get sick from their diet as well as through everything that their senses perceive and make humans sick, limited, governable and above all consumerist. .

Ideas are distorted according to the interests of the individual, his fixations and spiritual pathologies, religious creeds are a human pathology, since instinct usurps reason, that is, reasoning free of prejudices and taboos is avoided.

Reason has tools to think well, illustrious human beings have a high range of reasoning, but they are not exempt from mental pathologies and vice or error.

Human life must be free of political and economic vices, free of coercion from other beings, failing to fulfill our duties should scare us more than the pressure that another entity exerts on ours. The chains that bind us are intangible, those chains are more difficult to break than material chains. In politics, actors dedicate themselves to acting using a script far from reality and the practices of the union, they offer a better world, when in reality they are a mafia and generate rapacious deceptions that turn humans into a cloud of darkness and hopelessness. .

The mind perceives only moments of reality and in an angular, determined, fixed and partial way, that is, they are only flashes of reality and depending on the mirror with which you see things, it generates an attitude and disposition towards that real phenomenon, from that mirror you interpret reality according to subjectivity. There are creeds that are induced, and we believe they are real, fears that have no foundation, mirages without reality, distorted memories, storage errors, versions that never existed. Therefore, we do not have full insights, only glimpses of reality and life experience. Therefore, there is no one who has that full mental health, much less full emotional health, the social being is an entity with vices, errors and pathologies, therefore, there is no one healthy, there is no one sane, crazy We all have a little, but most of us possess the ability to maintain a balance, however, we are not taught to think or to seek balance between mind, body, spirit and heart.

The word trap

When the heart speaks the soul listens, when the mouth speaks only the ears hear, the word is the most sacred thing in total creation, it does not mean that God said and it was done, no. The word is much more creative than reality itself. From the logos arises the idea and from the idea arises everything that exists, however, the vulgar and ordinary word is a trap.

They use the trap of the word as a means of deception to obtain satisfaction for human vices, how many traps we hear in all spaces on earth, in all social networks and means of human interaction, the human word is deceptive and therefore so much a trap. Don't believe what you hear, listen to the voice of reason, the constant and deceptive word sounds in our minds but we rarely hear the pure and transparent word, that word outside of error.

In ancient times the philosophers directed their speech, but many of them were to lead the masses to their creeds and small vision of the world, however, the pure word still remains and emerged from some of them as universal knowledge, we then have wisdom. of these beings that have not yet died and are valid in our days.

In our reality, which is spiraling and regressive like a true labyrinth trap, things never end, they transform. Matter is a container of energy and these are never destroyed, the change of things is designed by the great architect who, through the logos or the word, gave existence to everything that exists, thus the word is the medium of the idea.

When we listen to a profane and ordinary being who uses the word to deceive another entity in order to obtain benefit through deception, we see the poverty of humanity and it is very common for beings to be addicted to lies, this is how we find conglomerations in temples, on terraces and at political rallies. Humans enjoy fallacies and generate false hope based on the lies that actors send to their ears, sweetening their ears and generating tainted interests.

In media technology we hear many traps every day that the purpose is to obtain a benefit from the masses, that is, the word is used to sell, to believe and generate false needs in the recipient. Then the recipient, in the need to be better, goes and buys the merchandise to feel valuable, this is a deception that costs lives and because of such consumerism we are devouring the planet, man has stopped being a wolf of man and has become a devourer. of everything that exists, that is, devourer of the planet.

Humanity will find a reform and a new codification of values to generate a new human, universal, without religion, without fanatic creeds, without policies of plunder and greed. When humans achieve a reform in their code of conduct, we will be able to ensure the survival of humanity, while we will live in anxiety, in the constant fear of becoming extinct.

The word liberates, but it also enslaves and at this moment we are slaves of lies, of fallacy, because there are evil beings who preach with a supposedly transparent and pure word, however, it is a dirty and dark word, thus we have those who speak of universal values, of ideals and sublime principles for humanity and the planet, however, his speech is dirty and tendentious, a trap. The word must be accompanied by example, if you say you love humanity, your actions must be directed toward doing good and always question what you do. When you hear a moralist, you laugh, because there are those who live from noble causes, which started with purity and end up making a business. Be careful when you hear one of those merolics speak who are in search of power, they are looking for nothing more than to hook you and make you their puppet.

Nowadays they use the distorted and silly word for spectacular purposes and to collect "likes" on social networks and at the polls. The word is devalued and poor, no one believes in anyone anymore because the lie or the wrong word has already been abused, ignorance does not allow us to conduct ourselves with the truth and with enough transparency to convince others that we are apostles of good word, that which is accompanied by good example.

The gods of all cultures use the word to make the coreligionists believe what they say their god said, but the word written in religious books includes vices of humanity, because they are written by humans themselves and then they give them the use to establish very profitable businesses, where the merchandise is god. That is why we are careful with the word that enters our senses and does not reach our deepest acceptance. Because faith blinds reason and a human without reason is not divine creation since pure reason is the creative being and we participate in it with material limitations, due to our nature.

The word transports us in time, unites the past with the present and prepares the future, those who transcend time are those who manage to develop ideas and use the word in a way that is close to the idea, however, the word is subject to interpretation, the latter can be as great as the understanding of the person who interprets it, understands it, meditates on it and develops it in reason. The word can be erroneous and carry error as a message over time, the word is often subject to change or development, depending on the truth that is accepted, that is the greatness and veracity of the word.

In ancient times the logos was the creative element, from it everything emanates, it is the creative principle, the origin of everything, when the word arises the thing is born according to religion, in reason the thing arises and the word arises, this is how it is printed in the essence of the word the essence of the thing, the essence captures it and transports it from entity to entity, but this arises with the encounter of the rational being with the thing, otherwise there cannot be any word, we find a diversity of languages and they are not the same, therefore the language is not finished, it is a result of the interaction and need to transmit ideas.

How many use the word in an evil way to obtain power, to subdue and manipulate races, how many use speech to generate ideologies, truths of political and economic interests, but not true statements of freedom, hope and love. The word is used with the purpose of obtaining a current that drags humanity to behaviors of imitation and alienation. Many media are used today to transmit the word with the purpose of bringing consumers to their business, the sender also functions as a guide for the receiver so that they do not make an effort to think, but rather live in the pleasure of alienation and consumption. Those who use the word with the intention of telling the truth distance themselves from human practice and are not welcomed into society as a persona grata, since humans are addicted to lies and falsehood.

You tell a human being the truth and it hurts more than losing an organ in their body, you tell them a lie and they are your friend forever, humans really like flattery and nice words full of praise and falsehood. In all systems of ideologies we find that the hermeneutics of their principles are subject to the whim of those who use them, in laws it is the same, in moral codifications it is also used at the whim and subject to the interests of those who use the word.

The word is that stimulus from the senses that travels to the central nervous system, generating a message and therefore resulting in an action. Always take care, the word as a sacred thing is the way to make ourselves known and to know the inside of people, the word is that window that allows us to see the light inside the individual or the darkness inside, the word is that river that flows from one being and reaches another, dragging with it hidden messages, not only sound waves, but it carries hidden messages that only the unconscious perceives, so when you speak, always try to be transparent and very careful that it adheres to healthy thoughts and feelings.

The word gives birth to the spirit and actions reveal the human spirit, so always take care of your being not to listen to perverse and manipulative beings, take care that your being always receives healthy messages without evil. Always reason and question the word you hear, do not be a sheep of the deceitful words of beings who do nothing but evil and harm to humanity, among these beings we find the political, religious, academic, economic and social currents. The word liberates or binds according to the interest of the issuer.

The compassion trap.

No being feels sorry for another without an interest, it may be the satisfaction of fulfilling his duty, it may be the satisfaction of his healthy intentions or the need to have satisfaction from the sweetness that comes from doing good. Whoever receives charity from another being feels grateful in the moment and whoever gives satisfies the need to feel good. But in reality, charity must be practiced without any interest, in a natural way and without interest in acquiring points for a better location next to the father, charity is a means to enslave the other when there is evil.

The one who gives often condemns the receiver to continue receiving, to not learn to generate, however, there are situations of people who fall from grace and are the ones who actually need compassion. Be careful of those who give in order to build empires, in this reality the charity of the powerful is a very profitable business, it can end with tax evasion or the search for points to win the political contest.

We find in this deceitful system charity as a business, that is, there are those who do million-dollar charitable works and then publish it in the newspapers with the greatest circulation and of course they document it and therefore deduct it from taxes, that is, charity serves as merchandise to achieve the ends of permanence in power, achieve power, maintain prestige and acceptance, charity is also used as that form of expression of power, marking the position between the strong and the weak, charity functions as a conduit of ideology of classes, so that those below are grateful to those above for how benevolent they are towards the weak. However, falling into that trap of accepting the divine and natural designs of accepting strong owners of the weak is the most vile and unnatural thing there is. Every human with a standard reasoning capacity is capable of achieving any challenge and, above all, being sensitive to the human race in an empathetic way. Equality is not achieved when you see less of someone, much less when you lose ground and your feet stop touching the ground. , that is, when the vices of the superego raise the entity to the clouds.

Charity is real when you give a smile and that smile manages to transform with its magic the emotional posture of the other, transporting them to a better state of mind, charity is when you give a gift without that old lady knowing your name and even more so without anyone seeing you, It would be like one of those kind pranks that no one plays, those pranks of doing good are not practiced by anyone. That charity that transforms the world into a different one, that must be practiced daily, it is better that they call us crazy and not criminals, since there is an abundance of models of compromising with others and receiving the title of great person, when in reality we find ourselves with a nefarious, perverse and evil being.

Compassion is a way of lowering ourselves to the level of someone who is experiencing a difficult situation and who are in the position of being able to practice compassion in an empathetic way. Human beings, when we see ourselves superior to anyone, feel great and stop being compassionate, not We manage to get down to the level of people and try to solve or improve the situation of others, compassion can be used altruistically, but many use compassion to achieve vanity and the title of kind.

At this point in time, ethics and morality are for people outside of normality, however, there are those who study to practice it and improve the human race, others use morality and ethics as a form of empire and obtain power, money and prestige. I mean religions. Humanity must strive to achieve a humanistic education, attached to ethical values and principles, practicing morality so that love reigns in humanity. We cannot maintain a gross savagery that makes the strong stronger and the weak sinks into its depths. misfortune. Those who are already successful seek in an excessive and stratospheric way the subjugation of humanity so that they increase their profits excessively.

Do not fall into the trap that moral and ethical principles are subject to the material, it is true that the importance given to the material is much greater than that given to the essences, to the spiritual aspect. The material cannot be superimposed on the spiritual because it breaks the harmony and we will experience the problems of today, where the material is more important, valuable and desired, leaving without value the world of values and spiritual aspect that has been left impoverished and without followers. , nor acceptance.

When the first thinkers tried to explain the world, they did so with myths, then it became discontinuous because a greater demand arose, with rigor and trying to satisfy those doubts of humanity that some have been moderately completed, but thought is subject to future and improvement. The values are always the same, they do not change and their practice will be universally accepted, that is why the wicked take advantage of this situation and use the ideals, values and principles to bring grist to their mill. Practice the values without knowing to whom and that will bring abundance and prosperity.

The trap of love.

Profane love is the trap of those in need of material things, the love of an apprentice of wisdom is the begging of light. He who truly loves will never trap another being to make it his own, but rather, he frees and makes a better being. Breaking the chains and bringing your loved one closer to independence is the way that a free being seeks to make other beings of the same condition. However, love is used as a trap, it is like the flower that traps the hummingbird and enervates it, making it addicted to its being. Love is not a possession, humans tie the beings that play at loving each other with ties and laws, then it becomes suffocating and the knots tighten day by day, it is like the dog that is tied to the bullring, it goes around and around until running out of rope and from so much pulling the noose bursts, leaving him free.

Love is the bait that some beings use to catch fortunes or achieve their human aspirations, however, love is transcendent, beyond what we can achieve without being prepared. To love we must be educated, if we are not educated for love, we cannot love, humans have the capacity to build themselves daily and their love must be coupled with their being, their actions and their existence itself, we cannot love without the universal ethical and moral principles.

In the era of excessive commerce, love becomes just another commodity; accessories are sold to encourage, grow or fake love. When you want to simulate love, a series of acts are carried out to stimulate a substance that gives the impression of love, but it is the trap, when one of the participants is not aware of the game, they fall into that trap, hurting their being. However, there are those who play the game of love and they knowingly play it, pretending to society an unmatched happiness, they pretend to be in a shelter of sweetness, however, it is just a game, a trap so that more victims play that game of love. falsehood.

Love is bitterness, sweetness and insipidity, the three modes in the three times and in the first, second and third person, you cannot achieve true love without sacrifice, without respect and without surrender. He who risks playing the game of true love faces many situations that can turn him into a free man or a slave to appearance, to mirage.

There are natural loves that are born without asking for them, without thinking about them, without even longing for them, it is the love of a mother with her derivative, the love of the species to preserve its existence, the love of a race for itself, it is accompanied by zeal and a selfishness, a rivalry, but at the same time an attachment to beings similar to oneself. Love is a project that carrying it out gives happiness and its opposition is failure, frustration, emptiness and bitterness, love goes to healthy beings, hate to sick beings, false love makes beings passionate, true love It makes them reasonable, it is not true that love and reason are opposites, those who love think very well, those who are passionate act on impulse without reflecting.

Love is a commodity that commercial beings sell and record on paper, it is trained to enter a frame and one cannot leave that frame, the churches handle it like that love that is beaten, scourged, crucified, tortured and painful, love is not It must hurt, love is tiring, but it is an accumulation of experiences, emotions and achievements.

The media trap.

Regardless of the lack of truth or precision of the media, what they do in the subconscious and conscious is impressive. If you have had communication equipment in regular use, you know that by receiving so many images, videos and information your Memory runs out and the system begins to fail, this is what happens in human memorization, processing and storage systems.

The subconscious is invaded by so much information that it cannot assimilate whether it is true or false and begins to send distorted information to the conscious.

When distorted information goes to the conscious, it becomes the executor of erroneous orders and can engage in frequent repetition of behavior such as the attachment to satisfy a false need that enslaves it to that need to satisfy that pleasure or attachment.

When the media bombards us with movie scripts, information and a vast amount of images that reach the brain and especially the subconscious, it atrophies because it cannot resolve and explain the material received. The problem is not to receive or invade a system and make it dysfunctional, but rather, the evil lies in the fact that this sick system will coexist with other systems and the disease is transmitted and becomes viral. At this point in humanity, the disease has already been naturalized. disease of unnecessary information to alienate the human mind and make it immune to conscience and moral principles. The unconscious human functions like animals, through instinct, that is, they go to work by instinct, they go to church by instinct, they go to live with friends by instinct, vice and by fashion. There are few clubs or institutions that promote austerity and living free from irresponsible use of media. Promoting awareness and the use of moral principles has been used as a business and not as a universal free-of-profit principle. Moralistic institutions put the economic factor before freely and selflessly proclaiming universal ethical values. Thus we find enormous monuments, states of gold whose fortune has been built based on deception and sale of divinities.

When they see themselves discovered or in danger, they unite against those who preach freedom of belief or freedom of thought, they run to make councils, canons, condemnations, prohibitions, persecutions and executions. The media enter into this ideological bombardment to channel people into an ideological, political, academic and cultural current but they will never allow you to think differently and above all to be free, free men and women are a thing of discredit, death or prison, there is no place for full and free humanity, it has to be subject to certain standards of behavior and thought already established.

This is how the system is determined and changing it is gradual, humans are very late to mature ideas in a general way, that is, the social being changes very slowly, but they are those great beings that set the tone for humanity as we see in history. . Be careful, there are also diabolical beings that condemn humanity to live in the petty system and prolong the life of that evil for many centuries. This is how empires move their troops and wage war against those who spread new ideas and freedom, making Entire nations die from blood, bacteria, viruses, ideology and hunger. Then it appears in history that they are the good ones, because they are the ones who write freely what they want to be known, for that they use the printed and digital media, repeating the lie millions of times until the naive person believes that lie or truths. socks.

The media, the production of books, magazines, newspapers, cinema, television, etc. It is a monopoly of empires to sustain lies, while those who have truths to tell crush them and build on their ruins, another imposing form of system.

The material trap.

We are educated to achieve comfort and pleasure, however, we ignore the spiritual, everything close has value and the deep, the essential has little value for the ignorant. In material life we look at what is material and it is the first impression we have when encountering the world, our experience is natural. First we encounter the thing that is printed or impresses us, then derived from it comes the idea that arises from a process of that encounter with the material; Giving an example of such a case, we mention the smile, first we find lips on a face that smiles, then we know that this expression is one of joy, a better example would be, we find fire, we touch it, then we will know that it burns, what I'm trying to say that symbology arises from experience and not the other way around. First is the impression and then the word, we cannot say that the word arises by itself or that it is autonomous, the idea precedes the word that is why we transmit ideas and although sounds link us with ideas or experience, the word is not before than the idea.

When we stay in the material stage is when everything we do revolves around the material and we become addicted to the material, accumulating everything possible without measure. There are those who accumulate material wealth for many of their generations, they are lucky, that's what they call them, but it is a material fortune, it does not mean that they have reached spiritual plenitude, that is why the rich hardly have love for humanity and for these universal precepts because It is so much their egocentrism and greed that they accumulate surplus value, this is the life of the worker, stripping him of his life and becoming fortune for a miser who in exchange for his happiness steals the human essence .

The freedom of matter is achieved through healthy instruction and the perennial education of the human being. Ignorance is a means that commercial and fashion trends use to drag and manipulate masses, that is why social struggles arise in defense of a louse, then the defense of those who defend the louse, and those who defend equality arise. sexual of the piojito, the piojita and the piojitae, this is just straw and commerce because they use the material to dominate the spiritual, the human will. For the same reason that we are not prepared to transcend beyond the material, but rather we remain in the foreground and from there we are caught in the material trap.

Charcoal in the thought trap

When we are born we come with instinctive ideas that help us survive, but they are still ideas, therefore, they have value and consideration to reflect on them, however, there are those who say that we are born as a blank slate, without any reasoning. Well, it may be true that existence at some point gives us reasoning and innate ideas. I mean that before we are born we are already carrying out acts of thinking, this with ideas according to the perceptions of our sense in function, however, returning to the blank slate, we can say that that table or rather that organ is filled with intelligent ideas. conscious and unconscious that throughout life we carry and give insight, although there are ideas that are kept in our subconscious and we do not bring them to light at any time. Thought can trap us in redundancy, like a vice or labyrinth with no exit, to get out we need a guide, with whom we can comment and receive guidance, sometimes the guide does not exactly have to be a human, the wind guides the aromas why not to let ourselves be guided by the masterpiece, by the voice of our fellow human beings, by the song of a bird, by the terror of the unknown, by the sweetness of a honeycomb and the pain of a bee. To guide our steps correctly in our thinking is to walk towards knowledge.

Thought is a door that makes us free or slaves, it frees us when we give way to pure knowledge that becomes wisdom, but it enslaves us if it traps us in prejudices and fanaticisms, when our knowledge is static and finished, at that point it is the jail, the trap. It should be said that one day Carboncito met an old friend who invited him to an old institution, where they taught how to build oneself, it is a space to study philosophy, at that moment when Carboncito was invited, it seemed new to him and generated very curious, but his desire was philosophy, so he got excited and began the trip to the old institution.

When they received him, Charcoal was blinded, with many conflicts and physical and moral vices, then the blindfolds fell from his eyes and he understood that light is received gradually until he obtains the light that guides him in his walk through the world, always measuring his steps. .

It is true that the fact of hanging out with free men gives you the desire to be free; when you live among vicious men, you will be a vicious being. In that academy I understood that delving into oneself is a painful act that makes you surprise and regret the imperfections of the human being. But the study of wisdom shows you the way to act with temperance in search of truth and justice.

Then the degree of knowledge comes slowly, without haste, but without pause, it is better to walk than run on the path of knowledge. Walking gives you the opportunity to reflect, running can dazzle and dazzle you, that is why time is a factor that we must know how to play with, when the capacity of the container is exhausted, the water drains away, generating waste of such a valuable liquid, knowledge is Likewise, we must pour enough into our capacity to discern, assimilate and approve, then go through various filters again until we reach the version that is close to the truth.

Carboncito traveled several paths and the best one was that of the academy that taught him to build himself, that academy that taught Beethoven melody, Marx taught him justice, Simón taught him freedom, Juárez taught respect, in short, many men and women who, upon leaving the academy, have made the difference between the profane and the symbolic in their lives.

This bunch of ideas, some unclarified, are out of necessity to say and not out of hope to be read, my works are not commercial and I doubt they will ever be on supermarket shelves, however, I am grateful for the freedom to express myself to those who They gave their lives to achieve such a vital right.

Among the struggle of opposites that reside within me, I manage to bring out slight sparks that I try to send to those who give me the opportunity to read me, your charcoal friend says goodbye to you, who is not a writer but a fan of the line.

About the Author

Juan Manuel Ramírez Magallón
Filósofo y abogado escritor independiente de Michoacán México